Momma's Gluten Free, Dairy Free & Sugar Free Cookbook

of Louisiana Classics and Southern Food Essentials

By J. W. YOUNG

Momma's Gluten Free, Dairy Free & Sugar Free Cookbook

of Louisiana Classics and Southern Food Essentials

By J. W. Young

DEDICATION

To
Hunter JG Young: You are the most
important person in my life. I love you!
Besides being an amazing kitchen and
editorial assistant, you are a genuine hero
and a real man. Thank you for saving my
life time and again. God loves you, too.
You kick ass, stunt man.

Also,
Joey Ramone—there's gluten-free pizza in
heaven.

FOREWORD

Gluten free, dairy free and sugar free eaters can get back in the good food game!

About Me

I am not a Chef. I am an Eater. At an early age, I was diagnosed with a lifelong chronic "no-cause, no-cure" disease called hidradenitis suppurativa (HS). I have struggled with it for over forty years. And, I hate tHis Shit! In my experience, the symptoms of the disease were triggered by my food choices. So, after eliminating some food options, I rediscovered how to eat and live and thereby lessened the challenging effects of the HS disease.

It's tough being food affected. Living with a food restriction in order to reduce the outbreaks of illness is not a fad for me. As a result, these are my eats. All the recipes are gluten free (GF), dairy free (DF) and without added sugar (SF) presented with sugar substitutes. I developed these recipes to satisfy my family's tastes— savory, spicy, fresh, and authentic—but this collection is adapted specifically for my food restrictions. These dishes stem from classic Louisiana cuisines and Southern cooking. So, let's eat and enjoy!

Get ready to scream for joy from the first taste and clamor for the last bite. *Momma's Gluten Free, Dairy Free and Sugar Free* recipes deliver a taste that you can't forget. Eat well and eat *free*.

Disclaimer

There are many types of diseases, allergies, sensitivities, cancers, and intolerances associated with food—and they are not the same. I am not a doctor. These are my personal experiences. Carefully seek professional answers. At the end of the day, enjoy life.

Contents

Terms and References

Large chopped is just about the size of a quarter.

Chopped is usually roughly the size of a nickel.

Diced (or small chop) is about half of medium chop, perhaps a quarter inch to a side.

Minced is very fine, as small as I can get it.

An asterisk (*) denotes a minimum recommendation.

Adjust to taste as you see fit. I personally tend to use double the garlic, herbs, and spices, but that's just me.

<u>RECIPE ESSENTIALS</u>

Cast Iron. A most essential cooking element—particularly for cooking gumbo, red beans, and jambalaya. Cast-iron pots and skillets can handle high-heat cooking. They are also traditionally used when cooking to feed big families. In fact, families still pass down their cast iron cookware to the next generation as an heirloom. Cast iron is naturally nonstick only if it has been seasoned correctly. Before the first use, be sure to season the cast-iron pan. I typically use the oven to do this. See the "Cooking Preparations" section for "How to Season Cast Iron" instructions.

Coconut Oil. Select a good quality, unfiltered, high-heat coconut oil. It adds a hint of coconutty sweet and a new depth of flavor to recipe essentials, like roux or for pancakes. If the coconut oil is liquid, you can simply pop it into the fridge and use it in the same way as a stick of vegan butter.

Coconut Cream. Without dairy to rely on, I use coconut cream as a substitute. Make your own by simply putting a can of coconut milk in the refrigerator overnight. Open the can and skim the cream that has separated from the milk. Use as suggested. It's also my favorite coffee addition.

Dairy Free. All of my recipes are dairy free by default. Simply put, it means excluding all the dairy products, including milk from any animal, plus butters, drinks, and cheeses that contain milk. In the grocery aisle, you may find food packaging marked "DF" on the product labels to indicate dairy free. Be careful, as some dairy-free prepared products may contain derivatives like whey or casein (which is a milk protein). Some products marked "nondairy" technically are allowed to contain a very small percentage of milk by weight. Buyers, be aware.

Dairy-Free Milk. I recommend cashew milk for a creamy sweet option. However, you can use any dairy-free milk you prefer, like hemp milk or almond milk. Making your own dairy-free milk is an easy best choice. I keep homemade seed and nut milks ready in the fridge as an alternative to dairy. Try my easy cashew milk recipe that follows in the "Starters" section, or use any type of nuts, seeds, or even oats if you prefer.

Dried Herbs. I process my garden bounty in the kitchen and make dried herbs. Unlock all the flavor of herbs by buying whole spice seeds or drying or dehydrating your own fresh herbs. Just add the whole dried ingredients to a blender or food processor. Now, your spice cabinet is ready and full flavored. I love making my own dried onion powders and dried chili spices for recipes. When the dust settles, store in an airtight container for long-lasting flavor.

European-Style Cultured Vegan Butter. This ingredient is at the heart of many *Momma's Gluten Free, Dairy Free and Sugar Free* recipes. No, not the sticky nut butter spread! A European-style cultured vegan butter product is one of the best replacements for sticks of real dairy butter. Cultured vegan butter is plant based and has been fermented with live cultures. Therefore, it melts, spreads, and tastes just like real butter. While you can find this product in many specialty stores, it **is not** a cheap item. Can't find it at your grocer? Don't worry, just substitute *solid coconut oil* whenever the recipe calls for *vegan butter*.

Dried Herbs, Spices, and Ingredients. Fresh is best! However, if using dry spices, these ingredients are pantry basics and easily found at local grocers. Be sure to reduce the fresh recipe amount used **by half**. For example, if the recipe calls for two tablespoons of parsley, then substitute one tablespoon of dried parsley.

A quick warning: Nowadays, dried herbs often lack quality and any found in the grocery aisles can be stale. As a result, the flavor is often diminished. There are also food safety and food fraud issues that are becoming widespread, where spices are often sold as inferior or mislabeled. Be cautious.

Fresh Herbs, Spices, and Ingredients. 'nuff said. This collection of recipes always calls for fresh herbs and spices, unless otherwise noted. If you have or have ever wanted a rooftop or window garden of herbs, by all means plant your own herb garden of Louisiana traditional essentials, like parsley, oregano, basil, thyme, or even bay leaves. Use fresh!

Gluten Free: The term "gluten" is a general name that refers to the protein found in some grains, which can be really unsafe for some free eaters. All of my recipes are gluten free by default. In the grocery aisle, you may find food packaging with "GF" marked on the product labels to indicate gluten free.

Gluten-Free Flour. My recipes use gluten-free flour exclusively. My go-to ingredient is BOB'S RED MILL Gluten Free 1 to 1 Baking Flour out of the many great ones on the market. I use it for all recipes contained in this book and in my daily eats. This is the easiest and best 1:1 substitution I have ever found. In addition, you can also use it in any recipe that calls for self-rising flour.

Most nuts and seeds can be made into gluten-free flour; however, they do not equally yield optimum results. I have had some success making recipe essentials, such as roux, with alternatives like brown rice flour. But, I cannot stress enough how <u>important</u> it is to use the correct gluten-free 1:1 flour as not every type of gluten-free flour works.

Louisiana Spice Blends. Many grocers carry spice blends that are typically marketed as Louisiana, Cajun, or Creole salts and seasonings. Try them out as you will likely find a favorite. Or make your own by blending garlic powder, ground cayenne pepper, paprika, dried parsley and salt. Homemade options are easy and will give you more flavor control—especially on the salt content.

Rice. Like Mardi Gras and its festivals, Louisiana's cuisine and rice dishes are famous around the world.

From celebrations centered on rice dressing and dirty rice to the essential one-pot meal—jambalaya. Louisiana is also one of the world's top rice producers. It all started with tiny seeds being tossed into the bayous and ponds, which returned rice harvest goodness.

We raise our dish to the grains of rice. Traditionally a medium-grain rice is used for Louisiana cooking—and, that is fine—just choose a variety that offers the fluffiness and lightness that you enjoy. I often use long grain rice for my favorite dishes when called for. Plus, I sometimes cook rice with veggie stock instead of plain water.

Roux. A crucial base ingredient for most savory, timeless Louisiana meals. This recipe starter is made from cooking flour and oil. Louisiana's cuisine already has a special blend of flavor, gentleness, and patience. Roux is no exception. It requires one to spend time making it, slowly sprinkling flour into oil, stirring continuously, and cooking it up into a smoky concoction.

See "Roux" recipe in the "Starter Basics" section.

Stock. My personal favorites are high-fat stocks. Fat carries flavor, so you want this as the basis of your soup and gumbos. For example, my favorite cooking variations are using a turkey stock to make gumbo and beef stock for black bean soup.

Sugar Free, Sugar Alternatives. Many foodies love, crave, or need sugar-free options, and all recipes in this collection emphasize using sugar alternatives and replacements. This will satisfy the cooking needs for those who must avoid sugar for personal reasons.

My favorite sugar alternatives ideal for cooking are monk fruit sweetener granules and allulose sugar substitute. Allulose is a naturally-occurring sugar found at low levels in certain foods, like figs, and is widely available as a sugar substitute.

Search the many available options for one that suits your personal taste. I typically mix the two types of granules for a balanced sweet flavor. There are also options for brown monk fruit sugar replacements. One of many brands that I like is KETOGOODS golden brown granules sugar replacement because it already blends the monk fruit and allulose.

Sugar-Free Honey. I truly appreciate all the new products on the market that feature monk fruit and allulose, especially when blended. High scores are given for products I really enjoy, such as WHOLESOME YUM Nature's Besti Zero Sugar Honey Substitute. It replaces honey 1:1 in every recipe that calls for traditional honey.

Trinity. Many Louisiana recipes call for a "trinity" of essential ingredients. The "trinity" references certain ingredient combinations from Louisiana cooking, which offer up a magical "*je ne sais quoi*"…meaning "I don't know what." It's just the "something special" that takes the flavor of a dish to a whole new level. This unique blend of three, or trinity, of ingredients is the key for spot-on classic cooking. The blends I typically use in my recipes are these:

- The holy trinity: Celery, bell pepper, onion
- Meat trinity: Sausage, chicken, shrimp
- Seafood trinity: Shrimp, crawfish, and crab

COOKING PREPARATION TIPS

à l'étouffée (like eh-too-feh). The technique used for cooking the aromatic vegetables is called à l'étouffée in French cooking. Some may refer to it as *sweating the vegetables*. Preparing many of these classic dishes in this way leads to soups and bisques with an incredible depth of flavor.

Sweating the vegetables à l'étouffée draws out the flavor. Simply do this:
1. dice your vegetables,
2. add a small amount of fat or oil to your pan,
3. put your prepared vegetables in a pot on low heat,
4. keep the lid on, and
5. let them cook slowly.

By keeping the lid on, you use the liquid to "sweat" (aka steam) them.

Blackening. This cooking technique involves coating protein, like fish fillets, in vegan butter with dried herbs and spices and then cooking in a very hot cast-iron pan for a short amount of time. It's like trying to get a smoky outdoor grill char on the meat but while cooking it in the kitchen. It will have a dark, crispy crust from simply being pan-fried. Don't burn it, blacken it.

Cooking with Induction versus Traditional Cooktops. Induction cooktops heat faster than electric burner or flame cooktops. Induction also offers improved efficiency and lower energy costs. Because induction cooktops create heat through pots and pans on the surface, I find that it can affect the overall cooking time for recipes. It is reported that induction cooktops can boil water 20-40% faster than gas and electric cooktops.

If you have made the switch to an induction cooktop, then it is very likely you will need to reduce the cook time stated in these recipes by 2-5 minutes per step or 10% less overall. If a recipe calls for cooking two hours, then reduce this time by about 24 minutes.

Lagniappe (lan-Yap). In old Louisiana tradition, if you visited the French Quarter of New Orleans, the shopkeepers would give you a small free gift as a thank you when you bought something.

In this cookbook, the word *Lagniappe* denotes a ***Cooking Variation*** where you may choose to add something extra and make it your own. It could be more flavor, additional ingredients, or spice and heat. When you see this word, get creative and add a little sumptin' that you can't explain. Enhance the flavor with a *little extra* that makes it taste just right.

Season a Cast-Iron Skillet. Cast-iron pans and skillets must be seasoned before first use and periodically thereafter. When you season the cast iron, it creates a nonstick coating. Some manufacturers preseason these at the factory.

To season a cast-iron pan at home, preheat the oven to 400F. Wash the cast iron skillet with a mild soap and hot soapy water, and then dry. Spread a thin layer of vegetable oil in the skillet. Use a towel to wipe out any excess. Place in the oven for about an hour. Carefully remove from the oven. When cooled, remove any excess oil with a towel. Over time and with lots of use, if the pan starts to stick, re-season the pan.

STARTER BASICS

Making Roux

When cooked, a roux should be the consistency of smooth peanut butter. If a recipe calls for "light roux," it will be a light-brown color like caramel. If a recipe calls for "dark roux," it will be the color of cocoa.

Make a large batch of roux in advance to save time later. Just adapt this recipe and increase the ingredients by whatever factor you want. Simply portion the roux into smaller measurements according to the recipe.

Essential Cooking Tips for Making Roux
1. Do not burn the roux! If it burns, start over with a new batch because it will ruin your recipes.
2. Store the cooled and prepared roux in a sealed jar for future use.
3. If the oil and roux separate when stored, just stir before use.
4. When using prepared roux, always follow the order. Add ***cold*** stock or water, and herbs and spices ***to*** the fresh hot roux.

Ingredients
2 ½ cups gluten-free flour, sifted (gradually add up to an additional 1 cup if of thin consistency)
1 cup vegetable oil, such as coconut oil

Roux Cooking instructions
1. Heat the oil in a cast-iron or heavy skillet over medium-high heat until it gets hot.
2. Sprinkle the flour into the pan about 1 cup at a time. The mixture should sizzle but not burn. Stir constantly.
3. Gently scrape the pan bottom to keep it from burning until the flour is dissolved in the oil.
4. Repeat until all the flour is added. The mixture should be bubbling and frothy at the top, so keep stirring constantly.
5. When the oil and flour mixture starts to turn light brown, reduce the heat.
6. If the roux is very liquid, add another ½ cup of flour. Sprinkle it in and continue to stir. If still thin after 20 minutes, add ½ more cup of flour. Keep stirring.
7. Continue cooking and stirring for 15 to 20 minutes to make a light roux or 30 to 45 minutes for a dark roux. It will turn a dark-brown color.
8. If you see small black specks floating in the pan, it is burning; switch to lower heat. If there are large black pieces, then it is burnt and you will need to start over with a brand-new batch.
9. When cooked, a thin layer of oil may float on the surface of the mixture. The cooked flour underneath should be the consistency of peanut butter or a paste. It should get harder to stir, and the stirring utensil should begin to resist in the pan.
10. Remove the pan from the heat and keep stirring for approximately 5 more minutes.
11. When completely cool, it will solidify. Store in an airtight container.

Stock

Prepare stock with food odds, ends, and scraps. Stock is
an essential ingredient and is used in nearly every recipe.
Try a poultry, wild game, or beef stock because these
meats give the finished stock such a robust depth of
flavor. Veggie stock with produce odds and ends is also
very useful.

Make a large portion ahead of time and separate into
smaller containers for use later on. Just store in an
airtight container and freeze. It stays good for several
months.

Ingredients
4 pounds meat scraps (add all the *bones, skin, and the
fats together*) *
4 quarts water
½ onion, chopped
4 sticks celery
4 tablespoons parsley, chopped
* Note: for veggie stock, use herbs and produce rough
cuts and end trims and add 2 tablespoons of coconut oil

Instructions
1. Add everything to a pot and cover with 4 quarts of
    water or more for a larger batch.
2. **For all types of stock, next add** the assortment of
    aromatic vegetables and herbs.
3. Add the fresh ingredients plus a few teaspoons of salt
    and some pepper. Season to taste.

4. Bring the mixture to a boil, then reduce heat and let simmer for approximately 4 to 6 hours to make the stock.
5. Strain to remove the whole cooked ingredients.
6. Let cool. Store in airtight container, then refrigerate or freeze.

Lagniappe Variation

Seafood stock is also just as easily made! Just prepare with whole fish or pieces, including the heads, and the shells if using crustaceans.

Cashew Milk

My all-time favorite dairy milk alternatives are cashew
and hemp milks. The homemade versions only keep well
for a few days. It's a great idea to pre-soak the nuts. I
find the end result is creamier without a presoak. Now,
let me share my secret ingredient while making cashew
milk or even cashew cream…it's the ice cubes.

Ingredients
1½ cups raw cashews
4 cups water
2 ice cubes
½ teaspoon vanilla extract

Instructions
1. Add all the ingredients to a blender.
2. Blend on "High" setting for 1½ to 2 minutes.
3. Strain twice and serve chilled.

Lagniappe Variation
Try using your favorite nuts like almonds. Make a
wonderful cashew cream by reducing the amount of
water to 2½ cups.

Pham Water

My Tai Chi instructor insisted I try this drink to encourage healing from the inside out. It's exceptional! Bird's-eye chilies are tiny, pointy red peppers when mature. Sometimes they are called Thai chilis at the market. Be sure to use gloves when handling fresh chilies.

Using a hot chili pepper in a drink may give you pause or the chilis may be hard to find. Just substitute dried cayenne pepper, as it is known to have antibacterial and anti-inflammatory properties. Remember, everyone is different; this is just what works for me.

Ingredients
1 to 2 bird's-eye chili peppers, ground with a mortar and pestle (or simply use ¼ teaspoon dried cayenne powder)
¼ teaspoon salt
16 ounces cold water
2 tablespoons lemon juice
2 tablespoons zero-sugar honey substitute or simple zero sugar syrup (see recipe)

Preparation
1. Empty all the ingredients into a tall glass.
2. Stir vigorously to blend. Strain to remove the solids.
3. Enjoy!

Spicy Sauce

One hot topper for a big dipper.

Ingredients
1 cup mayonnaise
½ cup hot sauce
1 dried Thai chili or spicy chili, ground
1 teaspoon lemon juice
½ teaspoon black peppercorns, ground
½ teaspoon parsley, minced

Instructions
1. Stir the dry, ground ingredients and mix well with the mayo.
2. Cover and store in the refrigerator.

Simple Zero Sugar Syrup

Simple syrup adds sugary goodness to iced teas, coffees, cocktails and other cold drinks. To prepare simple zero sugar syrup, choose a sugar alternative that is suitable for cooking, such as monk fruit sweetener granules.

Ingredients
2 cups water
2 cups monk fruit sweetener granules or a monk fruit and allulose blend

Cooking Preparation
1. In a saucepan, combine the water and sweetener.
2. Bring to a boil over medium heat. Stir to dissolve the sweetener.
3. Simmer for 5 minutes or until completely dissolved. Stir occasionally.
4. Remove from the heat.
5. Let cool completely.
6. Combine with your beverages of choice.
7. Store the remainder in a sealed glass container and keep in the fridge.

Lagniappe Variation
To make a rich simple zero sugar syrup, use a 2:1 ratio of sweetener to water. Infuse your simple syrup by adding spices or fruits, such as 1 vanilla bean (split) or 1 tablespoon fresh minced ginger before cooking. Discard the solids when you're finished cooking and before use.

CLASSIC MEALS

Momma's Signature Gumbo

This recipe is a mind-blowing take on a bowl full of Louisiana tradition. The smooth and smoky taste of the dark roux is what really makes this dish. A "holy trinity" combination of veggies and hearty meats is a must.

When I started my culinary journey, I had no idea what to cook for my native Louisiana family members. I got on the phone with someone who shared tips for authentic Louisiana cooking while laughing warmly. They finally said to me, *"Okay, try dis n' dat. One's a dish fuh' when ya po', d'uddas fo' when ya not!"*

Gumbo was *"d'udda."* Momma's recipes have evolved quite a bit over the years since. I hope you find my version is bursting with unforgettable flavor. This dish features my favorite trinity variations and it warms your life. When cooked, it should be a hearty but soupy stew.

Ingredients
1 cup gluten-free dark roux
2 green bell peppers, large chopped
1 yellow onion, large chopped
1 white onion, large chopped
3 stalks celery, chopped
½ head of garlic, diced
6 quarts cold stock or water
3 tablespoons oregano, chopped
3 tablespoons basil, chopped
3 tablespoons parsley, chopped
3 tablespoons garlic powder

2 tablespoons cayenne pepper, ground
½ teaspoon shrimp paste or dried shrimp, minced
¼ cup Louisiana spice-and-salt blend or seasoning
2 bay leaves, whole
6 pounds chicken leg quarters (or whole bone-in, skin-on, and cut into serving pieces)
1½ pounds smoked andouille link sausage (try beef or chicken)
1-pound fresh, peeled and deveined raw shrimp
Chopped parsley and green onion tops (for garnish)
Cooked rice

Instructions
1. Add the dark gluten-free roux to a large stock pot.
2. Melt the roux over medium heat. Stir gently.
3. When the roux begins to sizzle, stir in the chopped vegetables.
4. Cover the pot with a lid. Sweat the vegetables for 2 to 3 minutes.
5. Add the cold stock or water and all the seasonings to the saucepot. Stir.
6. Use a suitable spatula to gently scrape the bottom of the saucepan to remove browned bits.
7. Turn up to high heat. When boiling, drop the chicken pieces into the saucepot pot.
8. Cover the pot with a lid.
9. Let cook for 3 to 5 minutes or until it returns to a boil.
10. Remove the lid and scrape the bottom of the saucepot to mix in any roux sticking to the bottom.
11. Immediately turn down to low heat. Cover with a lid.

12. Let cook for 1 hour. The gumbo should be bubbling while cooking on a very low slow boil.
13. When the chicken pieces are floating in the pot, add the sausage. Cover with a lid.
14. Continue to cook on a low boil until the sausage floats to the top (about 30 minutes).
15. If the finished gumbo is thin or soupy, stir in 4 to 5 more tablespoons of the prepared dark roux.
16. Turn up the heat to medium-high and when the gumbo starts to boil more rapidly, add the shrimp.
17. Immediately turn down to medium-low heat. Cook for approximately 10 minutes more or until the shrimp are pink, floating and fully cooked.
18. Turn off the heat and remove from the stove.
19. Let cool.
20. To serve, add cooked rice to individual bowls. Ladle portions of the gumbo around the rice.
21. Sprinkle with parsley and green onion tops to garnish.

Lagniappe Variation

Remember, if the recipe calls for fresh herbs, you can always substitute dried herbs but half the amount needed. Also, you can try another meat trio of Momma's— smoked venison sausage, chicken and shrimp. My most favorite seafood trinity is truly a knockout punch…with shrimp, crab and crawfish!

Red Beans and Rice

Cooking red beans and rice on Monday in New Orleans is a cultural tradition, a phenomenon of sorts. It stretches back centuries and is as common as Mardi Gras. A staple among Louisiana families on Mondays—the traditional washing, cleaning and cooking day—was red beans and rice, which was left to simmer gently on the stove, all day, while the chores were being done. This filling dish and full meal sets you correct at the end of a long, hard day. Pick up a bowl—and, if it's good to you, then echo the locals by saying, *"Yeah, u rite!"*

Ingredients
1-pound small red beans
Water (twice the amount of the beans for soaking)
1 medium yellow onion, chopped
1 medium white onion, chopped
1 bell pepper, chopped
½ head of garlic, chopped
½ tablespoon basil, minced
½ tablespoon oregano, minced
½ tablespoon parsley, minced
½ tablespoon thyme, minced
1 tablespoon cayenne pepper, ground
3 tablespoons Louisiana salt-and-spice blend or seasoning
Stock or water (enough to cover the beans for cooking) +
1 cup reserved
1½ pounds smoked sausage
Chopped fresh parsley or dried parsley (for garnish)
Cooked rice

Instructions

1. In a large pot, sort and wash the beans, then drain. Remove any stones or debris.
2. Add the plain water to twice the height of the beans.
3. Cover the pot with a lid and soak overnight.
4. Drain any excess water.
5. Add all the chopped vegetables, herbs, and spices to the pot.
6. Add the stock or water to 3 inches above beans.
7. Turn on to high heat and bring to a boil. Immediately reduce to low heat and simmer.
8. The beans should barely be bubbling and always cooking on a very slow boil.
9. Continue to cook for 4 to 6 hours until the beans are soft.
10. When the beans start to stick to the bottom of the pot, add 1 cup of the stock or water. Scrape the bottom with a utensil and stir.
11. Cook for 30 more minutes.
12. When the beans start to stick again, use a potato masher and smash the beans (about ½ of the pot).
13. Add the sausage to the pot and add another 1 cup of the stock or water.
14. Cook on low heat for 20 minutes or until the sausage is cooked.
15. Remove from the heat and cool.
16. Serve over cooked rice in individual bowls.
17. Sprinkle with green onion tops to garnish.

Momma's Shrimp and Crawfish *étouffée*

For this classic dish, you've got to sweat the technique!

Check out the how-to à l'étouffée in the section.
"Cooking Preparation Tips." For this étouffée recipe we
will NOT be using a prepared roux; always make it
fresh. This is one recipe where I specifically seek out the
European-style cultured vegan butter product. To serve
this dish, cascade it lovingly over cooked rice..

Ingredients
7 tablespoons European-style cultured vegan butter or
coconut oil
1 tablespoon gluten-free flour
½ onion, diced
½ bell pepper, diced
2 ribs celery, diced
1 head of garlic, diced
3 cans stewed tomatoes with chilies; drain liquid but
reserve
1 tablespoon cayenne pepper, ground
1 tablespoon white pepper, ground
2 tablespoons salt
½ tablespoon dried shrimp, minced
½ teaspoon monk fruit sweetener granules
2 cups shrimp stock
1-pound raw, peeled, and deveined shrimp
½ pound raw, peeled, and deveined crawfish
2 tablespoons fresh parsley, chopped for garnish
½ cup green onion tops, thinly sliced for garnish
Cooked rice

Instructions

1. Prepare the onion, bell pepper, and celery and place in a separate mixing bowl. Set aside.
2. Strain the canned tomatoes and save the liquid in a small bowl.
3. In a large pan, heat 4 tablespoons of the European-style cultured vegan butter over medium-high heat. Add the tablespoon of gluten-free flour.
4. Keep stirring continually for 3 minutes until the mixture turns a light blonde color. Do not burn.
5. Add 1 tablespoon of the European-style cultured vegan butter to pan. Let it sizzle.
6. Immediately add the onion, bell pepper, and celery to the pan and stir into the roux.
7. Next. cover the pot with a lid, *à l'étouffée*, or "sweat" the vegetables in the mixture until they are clear or translucent. Cook for approximately 3 minutes.
8. Add 1 tablespoon of the European-style cultured vegan butter to the pan and stir until melted.
9. Use a suitable spatula to gently scrape the bottom of the saucepan to remove the browned bits.
10. Add the diced garlic. Stir to cook for approximately 1 minute.
11. Add the drained tomatoes to the pan. Turn up to high heat for 2 minutes, then return to medium-high heat.
12. Stir in the dry peppers, salt, and dried shrimp. Reduce the heat to the low setting and cook for 5 minutes.
13. Add the juice drained from the stewed tomatoes with chilies. The mixture will sizzle.
14. Turn up to high heat and when boiling cook for 5 minutes. Stir in the sweetener.

15. Reduce the heat to low and simmer for 10 minutes.
16. Stir in the stock. Turn up to high heat again and when boiling, cook for 5 minutes.
17. Reduce the heat to the low setting and simmer for 10 minutes.
18. Add the shrimp and crawfish to the pan. Stir.
19. Turn up to high heat, and when boiling, cook for 3 minutes. Reduce the heat to low and simmer for 5 minutes or until the shrimp is pink and cooked.
20. Remove from the heat and stir in 1 tablespoon of the European-style cultured vegan butter. Let cool.
21. Serve over cooked rice.
22. Sprinkle with fresh parsley and green onion to garnish.

Lagniappe Variation
Try chicken, vegan shrimp, or any of your favorite proteins.

Momma's Signature Jambalaya

This dish is a potent mix featuring a Louisiana "holy trinity" of ingredients along with a showcase of yet another—the meats! Bursting with sausage, chicken and fresh shrimp, we've got a lot going on with this dish. It's certainly Momma's signature meal and family favorite at mealtime.

Ingredients

5 tablespoons European-style cultured vegan butter or coconut oil, plus 1 reserved
½ onion, large chopped
½ green bell pepper, large chopped
2 ribs celery, minced
1 head of garlic, minced
1½ pounds boneless skinless chicken thighs, diced into 1-inch pieces
½ pound smoked sausage, cut into ½-inch slices
2 teaspoons cayenne pepper, ground
1 tablespoon Louisiana spice blend or seasoning
1 teaspoon parsley, chopped
1 teaspoon cayenne pepper, ground
1 teaspoon black pepper, ground
½ teaspoon dried shrimp, minced
¼ tsp dried gumbo filé (optional)
1 bay leaf
1½ cup uncooked long grain rice
3 cups stock
½ pound deveined raw shrimp, dried on paper towel. Sprinkle with salt and pepper.

Instructions

1. Turn on the heat to the medium-high setting.
2. Add European-style cultured vegan butter or coconut oil.
3. Add the bell peppers and stir 1 minute.
4. Add the onions stir for 1 minute, put a lid on the pot and sweat the vegetables in the oil mixture until the onions are clear or translucent.
5. Remove the lid and add the garlic and celery, stir for 1 minute. The mixture should still be sizzling.
6. Cover the pot to sweat the veggies again. Cook for 2 minutes.
7. Remove the lid. Remove the vegetables from the pan.
8. Return the pan to the stove on medium high heat and add the chicken pieces to the center of the pan.
9. Sear the chicken pieces for about 3 minutes.
10. When the chicken browns slightly, add the smoked sausage.
11. Pour in the uncooked rice and vegetables.
12. Add the dried shrimp and all dry spices and seasonings.
13. Add stock, stir, and scrape the bottom while adding to the pot.
14. Turn up to high heat and bring to a boil.
15. When boiling, immediately turn down to low heat. Add shrimp (do not stir).
16. Cover the pot with the lid. Simmer for 20 minutes or until liquid is evaporated.
17. Remove from the heat. Gently fluff with a fork and carefully fold the rice over the shrimp 2 to 3 times to ensure they are completely covered by the cooked rice.

18. Let stand for 5 minutes without the lid.
19. Remove the bay leaf. Let cool completely before serving.
20. Sprinkle with the parsley and green onion tops to garnish.

Lagniappe Variation

Don't hesitate to mix up your own seafood trinity…try crawfish, blue crab and shrimp! My family is left speechless when I substitute smoked chicken sausage for beef sausage in this recipe.

Blackened Fish

"Blackening" is a cooking technique that is popular in Louisiana. Any type of fish fillet would certainly work for this recipe, from redfish to catfish or bass. This technique is crucial and gives the protein a serious locked-in flavor.

The use of dried herbs is the key to achieving blackened perfection and unlocks the deep flavors of this seafood classic.

Traditionally a cast-iron skillet is used. Because we will be cooking at very high heat, I tend to use coconut oil for this recipe. The oil will be smoking hot; don't be concerned, just don't burn the fish.

Ingredients
¾ cup of European-style cultured vegan butter or coconut oil, melted. Plus, add 4 more tablespoons for frying.
3 tablespoons paprika, ground
1 tablespoon salt
1 tablespoon garlic powder
1 tablespoon cayenne pepper, ground
1 tablespoon onion powder
1½ tablespoon black pepper, ground
1½ teaspoon dried basil
1 ½ teaspoon dried thyme
2 pounds of fish fillets; dry off fillets on paper towels

Instructions

1. Add the dry spice ingredients to a large mixing bowl and set aside.
2. Heat a cast-iron pan over medium heat and add the European-style cultured vegan butter or coconut oil.
3. Stir the vegan butter or coconut oil until melted.
4. Pour the melted vegan butter or coconut oil into a large mixing bowl.
5. Pierce the ends of the catfish fillets with forks or use tongs to dip the dry fillets into the melted vegan butter or coconut oil. Coat both sides.
6. Place the dipped fillets into the dry spice mix and turn over to coat both sides. Set aside.
7. Heat the remaining vegan butter or coconut oil in a large cast-iron skillet.
8. Set the temperature to medium-high heat and slowly get the vegan butter or coconut oil very hot. The oil should turn brown and may begin to smoke.
9. Shake off the fillets to remove some of the spice mix before adding the fillets to the skillet.
10. Carefully place the coated catfish fillets into the hot vegan butter or coconut oil.
11. Cook each side approximately 3 minutes (until opaque) and turn over only once to cook another 3 minutes. The cooked pieces should have a dark crust on each side.
12. Remove the fillets from pan.
13. Serve immediately with fresh vegetables or over rice.

Southern Fried Shrimp

Get a few extra napkins ready for this one! The crunchy corn meal crust is a standout and the savory spices are magical. Stuff these morsels into a gluten-free baguette with Spicy Sauce (see recipe), lettuce, and tomato for the perfect Louisiana favorite—a po' boy sandwich!

Search the grocer's case for a gluten-free option. One I truly enjoy is UDI'S Gluten Free French Baguettes. What's even better? These golden gobs are versatile. Toss the cooked pieces on a salad for a light, healthy approach to good eats.

Ingredients
1-pound raw shrimp, peeled and deveined
1 egg white
½ cup cornmeal
¼ corn flour
¼ cup cornstarch
1 tablespoon salt
1 teaspoon garlic powder
1 teaspoon onion powder
½ teaspoon dried paprika
½ teaspoon black pepper, ground
½ teaspoon dried parsley
¼ teaspoon cayenne pepper, ground
½ cup dairy-free milk, like coconut or cashew milk
2 cups coconut oil, for frying
Spicy Sauce (see recipe) for dipping

Instructions

1. Rinse the shrimp and let dry on a plate lined with a paper towel. Lightly sprinkle with a pinch of salt and pepper. Set aside.
2. Add the egg white to a small mixing bowl and whisk until fluffy.
3. In another mixing bowl, blend the cornmeal, flour, cornstarch, salt, and the dry powders.
4. Add the dairy-free milk to the egg whites. Whisk until frothy.
5. In three steps, first dredge the shrimp into the flour mixture, then dip into the egg mixture and toss the shrimp back into the small bowl with the flour mixture until coated.
6. Remove the shrimp from the bowl and shake gently to remove excess powder.
7. Set up for frying in a Dutch oven or cast-iron skillet with high sides. Heat the oil to 350°F (about 10 minutes).
8. Working in batches, carefully add the shrimp to the hot oil. Cook until golden brown, turning once, about 2 minutes on each side.
9. Add the coated shrimp to the hot oil and fry for 4 to 6 minutes or until golden brown and firm.
10. Remove the cooked shrimp from the heat and transfer to a plate lined with a paper towel or cooling rack.
11. Let cool.

Momma's Favorite Fried Chicken

Head to the kitchen and make this great solution. What makes this dish unforgettable is the sweetness of the corn coating plus the coconut oil for frying. I cannot explain how it levels up the yum factor! That corn coating really makes this recipe one of my most treasured Southern dishes. Drizzle the zero-sugar honey substitute over the cooked chicken pieces for an unexpected *savory* sweet bite.

Ingredients
1 whole chicken, approximately 6 to 8 pounds, cut into pieces
½ cup salt for brine
6 quarts of water (to soak chicken pieces)
1 cup gluten-free flour
2 tablespoons cornstarch
2 tablespoons garlic powder
2 tablespoons onion powder
1 tablespoon salt
1 tablespoon paprika
½ tablespoon cayenne pepper, ground
1 teaspoon of each: dried sage, celery salt, thyme
1 teaspoon of each: basil, oregano
1 cup dairy-free milk, like coconut or cashew milk (see recipe)
3 egg whites
2 cups of crushed cornflakes
4 tablespoons zero-sugar honey substitute (optional)
2 quarts coconut oil, for deep frying

Instructions

1. In a very large dish, make a brine by mixing ½ cup of the salt with 6 quarts of water.
2. Soak the chicken pieces in the salt brine overnight or for at least 8 hours before cooking.
3. Remove the chicken pieces and dry on a paper towel.
4. Sprinkle 1 tablespoon of salt directly onto the chicken pieces. Set aside.
5. Prepare the dry seasonings. Blend them together. Take half of this mixture and sprinkle on the chicken pieces.
6. Save the other half to add to the flour mixture.
7. Set up a dredging station. In a small bowl, mix the flour, cornstarch and remaining half of the dry spices. Set aside.
8. In another small mixing bowl, add the dairy-free milk and eggs. Whisk until frothy and set aside.
9. Add the crushed cornflakes to a plastic bag and set aside.
10. Dredge the chicken. One piece at a time, dip the chicken piece into the flour mixture, then add it to the egg mixture. Next, add the piece to the bag of corn flakes and shake it to completely coat the chicken.
11. Place the coated chicken on a rack and repeat for the remaining pieces.
12. Set up for frying in a Dutch oven or cast-iron skillet with high sides. Heat the oil to 350°F (about 10 minutes).
13. Line a baking sheet or platter with paper towels or a prepare a cooling rack.

14. Add 3 to 4 chicken pieces to the oil and fry. Do not crowd the pan.
15. Use tongs to rotate the pieces every 4 to 5 minutes while adjusting the heat to maintain the temperature while cooking.
16. Cook until golden brown to an internal temperature of 165°F (insert a cooking thermometer into the thickest part of the chicken piece).
17. Use tongs to remove the chicken pieces from the hot oil.
18. Transfer the chicken to the paper-towel-lined pan or cooling rack.
19. Add the next batch of pieces and repeat the frying.
20. Let cool before serving.
21. Drizzle the chicken pieces with zero-sugar honey substitute if a sweet touch is desired.

Chicken Fried Steak

Here is another unforgettable deep-fried Southern classic
dish twisted for the free eater. A breakfast favorite for
everyone. My little ones love steak fingers! Just start by
slicing cube steak into 1-inch strips.

Ingredients
2 tablespoons salt
2 tablespoons garlic powder
2 tablespoons onion powder
1 tablespoon cayenne pepper, ground
1 tablespoon paprika
2 teaspoons dried parsley
1 teaspoon oregano
4 beef cube steaks, cut in half to make 8 pieces
½ cup gluten-free flour
2 tablespoons cornstarch
1 cup dairy-free milk (see recipe)
3 egg whites
1½ cups of crushed cornflakes
2 quarts coconut oil, for deep frying

Instructions
1. Prepare the salt and dry seasonings. Blend them
    together in a small mixing bowl.
2. Take half of the seasoning mixture and sprinkle on
    the beef cube steak pieces. Set aside. Save the other
    half to add to the flour mixture.
3. Set up a dredging station. In a small bowl, mix the
    flour, cornstarch and remaining half of the dry spices.
    Set aside.

4. In another mixing bowl, add the eggs and dairy-free milk. Whisk until frothy and set aside.
5. Add the crushed cornflakes to a gallon-size plastic bag and set aside.
6. Now you will dredge the beef cube steaks one piece at a time. First, dip the beef cube steak piece into the flour mixture, then add it to the egg mixture. Next add the piece to the bag and shake it to completely coat the beef cube steak.
7. Place the coated beef cube steak on a rack and repeat with remaining pieces. Set aside.
8. Set up for frying in a Dutch oven or cast-iron skillet and heat the oil to 350°F (about 10 minutes).
9. Line a baking sheet or platter with paper towels or a prepare a cooling rack.
10. Add 2 to 3 beef pieces to the oil and fry. Use tongs to rotate the pieces every 4 to 5 minutes, adjusting to maintain temperature while cooking.
11. Cook until golden brown to an internal temperature of 165°F (insert a cooking thermometer into the thickest part of the beef cube steak piece to measure).
12. Use tongs to remove the beef cube steak pieces from the hot oil.
13. Transfer the steaks to the paper-towel-lined pan or cooling rack.
14. Add the next batch of pieces and repeat frying.
15. Let cool before serving.

Lagniappe Variation
For vegan love, substitute meat protein with extra firm tofu and use an egg substitute. Start by freezing a block of extra firm tofu in advance. Thaw, then gently press

with paper towels to remove liquid before use. Cut into
½-inch slices or thicker. Add to a shallow dish before
marinating. While dredging, the pieces are delicate and
may crumble. Do not use a gallon size bag for coating,
just sprinkle the cornflakes on each side then gently
press. Arrange the coated tofu pieces on a plate and place
in the refrigerator for about 5 minutes before frying.

Buffalo Chicken Strips

A great snack pastime and fun food option. Every meal time is the right time for these tasty crunchy tenders.

Ingredients
3 pounds boneless skinless chicken breast or thighs, cut into strips
½ cup hot sauce
1 tablespoon cayenne pepper, ground
1 tablespoon onion powder
1 tablespoon garlic powder
1 tablespoon salt
2 teaspoons dried parsley
1 cup gluten-free flour
1 cup of cornflakes, crushed
½ cup cornstarch
1 egg white
Oil, for frying

Instructions
1. Mix the boneless strips, hot sauce, all dry seasonings, herbs, and salt in a large mixing bowl.
2. Cover with plastic wrap and let marinate for 4 hours or overnight.
3. In a small mixing bowl, combine the gluten-free flour, cornstarch, and cornflakes.
4. In another mixing bowl, add the egg white. Whisk until frothy.
5. Remove the strips from the marinade and dip into the egg white.
6. Dredge the strips one at a time into the flour mixture.

7. Shake to remove excess flour.
8. Place the coated strips on a rack. Set aside.
9. Set up for frying in a Dutch oven or cast-iron skillet with high sides. Heat the oil to 350 °F (about 10 minutes).
10. Line a baking sheet or platter with paper towels or prepare a cooling rack.
11. Add the strips to the oil and fry. Use tongs to rotate the pieces every 2 to 3 minutes, adjusting the heat to maintain the temperature while cooking.
12. Cook until golden brown.
13. Use tongs to remove the strips from the hot oil.
14. Transfer the strips to the paper-towel-lined pan or cooling rack.
15. Add the next batch of pieces and repeat the frying.
16. Let cool before serving.

Lagniappe Variation

Substitute the hot sauce with zero-sugar honey mustard substitute for a different, milder flavor. Vegan eaters may substitute thawed extra firm tofu as the protein and use an egg substitute. Gently press the thawed tofu block with paper towels to remove liquid and slice ½ inch or thicker.

Transfer to a shallow dish before marinating. The pieces are delicate and may crumble, so handle with care. Instead of dredging in the flour mixture, just sprinkle on each side then gently press. Arrange the coated tofu on a plate and place in the refrigerator for about 5 minutes before frying.

BREAKFAST EATS

Pancakes

Free the pancakes! Have a hearty breakfast meal made simple with a few kitchen staples. The baking powder is responsible for making these pancakes to rise, so it helps to aerate the batter well with a whisk. After mixing, always rest the batter for about ten minutes. This gives the baking powder time to activate.

A cast-iron skillet is my cooking utensil of choice here because it heats well and browns the pancakes without an excess of cooking oil. I also prefer to use coconut oil. A nonstick pan or griddle can be used too.

This is another recipe where I highly recommend the European-style cultured vegan butter for topping, as it melt and tastes like dairy butter.

Ingredients
1½ cups gluten-free flour
3½ teaspoons baking powder
1 tablespoon monk fruit sweetener granules
1/8 teaspoon cinnamon
1¼ cups water (add more for thinner pancakes)
3 tablespoons oil
Simple zero sugar syrup (see recipe, for topping)
European-style cultured vegan butter and berries
(optional, for topping)

Cooking Instructions
1. In a large bowl, sift together the flour, baking powder, sweetener, and cinnamon.
2. Make a well in the center and pour in the water, egg and melted oil. Mix until smooth.
3. Heat a lightly oiled cast-iron skillet, griddle, or frying pan over medium high heat.
4. Pour the batter into the skillet or on the griddle, using approximately ¼ cup for each pancake.
5. Brown on both sides for 3 to 5 minutes. Bubbles should appear on the surface of each pancake.
6. Remove from the pan and serve hot.
7. Top with the European-style cultured vegan butter, berries, and zero sugar syrup.

Apple Breakfast Sausage

Homemade sausage has been a joy to make since I stood side-by-side with my grandmother to prepare it. The sweetness of the apple is my favorite, as she used to call me the apple of her eye.

Ingredients

2 tablespoons oil
½ red apple, thinly sliced and diced
1-pound ground turkey or plant-based meat
2 tablespoons zero-sugar honey substitute
1 teaspoon salt
¾ teaspoon dried sage
½ teaspoon black pepper, ground

Instructions

1. In a small pan, melt 1 tablespoon of oil the over medium heat. When it starts to sizzle, add the apples. Stir and sauté for 5 minutes.
2. Remove from the heat and set aside to cool
3. In a mixing bowl, add the ground meat, zero-sugar honey substitute, salt, sage, and black pepper.
4. Add the apples with melted oil to the mixing bowl.
5. Use a fork to roughly stir the mixture.
6. Form the mixture into 2-inch balls and then press to make patties.
7. Melt 1 tablespoon of oil in a frying pan over medium high heat.
8. Add the patties to the pan and cook for about 5 to 7 minutes.
9. Flip the patties over to cook on both sides until done.
10. Remove from the pan to let cool. Serve.

Breakfast Sausage Potatoes

Here is my favorite breakfast recipe delivering the savor, the flavor, and the kick! Shift your breakfast into high gear with the classic seasonings of the South. Prefer vegan? You're in here. The grocery aisles are chock full of ground plant-based sausage options. Just be cautious and read the labels for any added gluten or dairy ingredients of concern.

Ingredients
4 large potatoes, diced
½ tablespoon salt
1 teaspoon onion powder
1 teaspoon garlic powder
1 teaspoon paprika
¼ teaspoon cayenne pepper, ground
4 cups oil for frying + 2 tablespoons
½ onion, chopped
½ bell pepper, chopped
1-pound smoked sausage links, cut into ½-inch pieces and quartered
4 cloves of garlic, minced (optional)

Instructions
1. Rinse and dice the potatoes. Set aside.
2. In a small mixing pot, add the salt and dry spices. Mix and set aside.
3. In large frying pan, melt the oil over high heat. There should be about 3 inches of hot oil.
4. Cook the potatoes in the oil until golden brown and floating.

5. Remove the potatoes and put them on a plate lined with paper towels.
6. In a large mixing bowl, toss the potatoes with the salt and dry seasoning mixture. Set aside.
7. In a small frying pan, heat 2 tablespoons of the oil over medium heat.
8. Add the onions, bell pepper, and sausage pieces. Stir to cook for 3 minutes.
9. Turn the heat to low, add the garlic if desired, and cook for 2 minutes.
10. Pour the veggie-and-sausage mixture over the fried potatoes and toss until well mixed.
11. Let cool before serving.

Lagniappe Variation
Spice it up! Use thinly sliced spicy peppers and cook with the garlic. For a savory dish, blend ¼ teaspoon of any variety of your favorite dried herbs plucked from your garden or pantry—like dill, basil, or sage.

Potato Patties

Honestly, exclusively eating gluten free and dairy free at breakfast usually sucks. But, by introducing potato patties to the rotation, the wake-up meal time is redeemed by these crunchy bites. These are my ultimate go-to. When the family reaches for their donuts, I just reach for potato patties.

You may want to double the recipe for a larger batch and cook ahead of time. You can use any frying oil; however, I prefer the subtle sweet and nutty flavor coconut oil adds to the patties. Store in a sealed container or freeze these appetizers. Potato patties are a very tasty and easy reheat treat!

Ingredients
4 large potatoes, shredded
½ onion, shredded
½ cup gluten-free flour
2 tablespoons cornstarch
2 tablespoons parsley, minced
1 tablespoon salt
1 teaspoon cayenne pepper, ground
¼ tablespoon black pepper, ground
2 large eggs
Oil for frying

Instructions

1. Shred the potatoes and onions into a large mixing bowl.
2. Add all the flour, dry ingredients, and eggs. Stir to mix well.
3. Heat the oil in a large frying pan.
4. Scoop ¼ cup of the potato mixture. Use two large spoons to form a mound, then press to flatten the balls into patties to fry up a crispier treat.
5. Drop the patties into the hot oil.
6. Fry 3 to 5 minutes or until brown and crispy.
7. Turn the patties over and continue to cook for 3 to 5 minutes.
8. The potato patties will float in the oil when done.
9. Remove from the pan and drain on a paper towel.
10. Let cool and serve.

Breakfast Bake

The first meal of the day is incomplete without a little
scramble in your life! The stand-out appeal of this dish is
how easy it cooks all-in-one in the oven. You'll be
surprised to find that many grocers now carry gluten-free
pie crust in the freezer case, ready-to-bake, in a prepared
8-inch pie pan. For this recipe, I typically use either a
chicken or vegan link sausage. Or, you can crumble in
the homemade apple breakfast sausage (see recipe). Try
out your favorites.

Ingredients
1 gluten-free pie crust, thawed
2 tablespoons oil
½ pound link sausage, cut into ½-inch slices and
quartered
8 slices of turkey bacon, cooked & chopped
8 whole eggs, whisked
½ teaspoon salt
½ teaspoon pepper
1 cup shredded dairy-free, vegan cheddar cheese

Instructions
1. Pre-heat oven to 350°F.
2. In a medium frying pan, add 1 tablespoon of the oil
    and melt.
3. Add the sausage links pieces and cook for 3 minutes
    over medium high heat.
4. Remove from the pan to cool. Set aside. Do not drain
    the oil.

5. Add the bacon to the pan and cook for 2 minutes over medium-high heat.
6. Remove the cooked bacon from the pan and cool.
7. Chop the bacon into pieces. Set aside.
8. Prepare the pie crust by spreading 1 tablespoon of the oil on the bottom.
9. Gently pierce the bottom of the gluten-free pie crust with a fork in 4 places.
10. Stir the salt and pepper into the eggs and whisk.
11. Pour the mixture into the pie crust.
12. Sprinkle the cooked crumbled bacon into the egg mixture.
13. Add the sausage slices.
14. Sprinkle the cheese.
15. Place the pan in the oven.
16. Cook for 30 to 40 minutes. To test for doneness, pierce the egg with a knife. If it comes out clean, then it is done. If the egg is moving or runny, cook for an additional 10 minutes and test again.
17. Remove from the oven. Let cool completely.
18. Slice and serve.

Little Man's Sandwich

There were many times when I traveled for work, so my son came up with recipes to make on his own—like this one. And, now that gluten-free bagels and dairy-free cream cheese are a regular option in the grocery aisle, I get to enjoy them, and so do you. Check the cold case for the bagels. And, if you have little ones, let them prepare these sandwiches on their own. They may even share.

Ingredients
1 gluten-free bagel
3 tablespoons no sugar added peanut butter
3 tablespoons dairy-free, vegan cream cheese
¼ cup fruit (i.e., banana, apples, strawberries, or any berries)

Instructions
1. Split the bagel and toast the inside.
2. Spread the peanut butter on one side.
3. Spread the dairy-free cream cheese on the other side.
4. Top one side with fruit.
5. Sandwich the breads together.

Enjoy!

ANYTIME EATS

Smoked Venison Chili

I tend to use a blend of dried peppers and fresh spicy
peppers. Wear disposable gloves when cutting spicy
peppers since the oils can burn the skin. Avoid touching
the face. Look forward to cold weather just so you can
make this dish. You can always substitute a turkey or
beef protein for the venison ingredient.

Ingredients
¾ cup black beans
¾ cup red beans
Water (double the amount of beans for soaking)
1 onion, diced
½ bell pepper, diced
½ head of garlic, diced
2 tablespoons spicy or mild chili powder
2 tablespoons of each: salt, cumin, garlic powde
1 tablespoon black pepper
3 tablespoons brown monk fruit sweetener
2 carrots, diced
2 tablespoons cayenne pepper, ground
2 spicy peppers, diced (such as jalapeño or serrano)
3 canned stewed tomatoes with chilis; drain liquid but
reserve
1 tablespoon oregano
3 tablespoons tomato paste
6 cups stock (to cover the beans for cooking)
½ pound of uncooked venison sausage, diced
1-pound fatty beef cut (such as brisket), cut into 1-inch
cubes
1-pound of each: ground venison, ground beef

Instructions

1. Lightly salt and pepper the beans to season prior to cooking. Set aside.
2. In a large saucepot, sort and rinse the dry beans then drain. Remove any stones or debris.
3. Add the plain water to double the height of the beans.
4. Cover the sauce pot with a lid and soak overnight.
5. Drain water to remove. Add all remaining ingredients to the stockpot **except** the sausage, beef cuts and ground meats.
6. Add the stock or water to the pot, until the liquid is 3 inches above the ingredients.
7. Turn on to high heat and bring to a boil. Immediately reduce to low heat.
8. Cover and let simmer for 2 hours.
9. The beans should barely be bubbling and always cooking on a very slow boil.
10. In a small frying pan, cook the beef cubes over medium-high heat just long enough to sear. Do not completely brown.
11. Pour all the partially-cooked beef cubes with its juices into the large pot.
12. Cook 2 to 3 hours until the beans start to soften.
13. Add the ground meats to the small frying pan and cook over medium-high heat just long enough to sear. Do not completely brown.
14. Stir the liquids and ground meats into the pot.
15. Cook for another 1 to 2 hours until the beans are very soft and the beef cubes shred with a fork.
16. Remove from the heat and let cool.
17. To serve, ladle into bowls and garnish with suggested toppings.

Lagniappe Variation
Garnish suggestions include chopped green onions, shredded vegan cheese, diced avocado or dairy-free sour cream.

Split Pea Soup

Green peas are packed with plant-based protein and fiber. Momma's earthy version is cooked and creamed to retain a little bit of texture. Yum!

Ingredients
1-pound dry green split peas
Water (enough to cover for soaking)
2 slices turkey bacon, diced
1 onion, diced
6 to 8 cloves garlic, diced
1/8 cup olive oil
¼ pound smoked sausage link, diced
8 cups stock or water (for cooking)
1 tablespoon of each: salt, pepper, garlic powder
1 teaspoon onion powder
½ teaspoon dried oregano
¼ teaspoon rosemary
2 bay leaves
2 sprigs thyme or ¼ teaspoon dried thyme
1 carrot, diced into ¼ inch pieces
1 rib celery, diced
1 potato, diced
1 tablespoon coconut cream, for serving (optional)

Instructions
1. Add the peas to a large bowl and cover with water.
2. Soak the peas for 10 minutes. Remove the skins floating on the surface. Drain. Set aside.
3. In a Dutch oven on medium heat, add a little olive oil to the pan and cook the bacon pieces until browned

and crisp. Remove the pieces but leave the rendered fat in the pan. Use the fat to sauté the onions for about 1 minute.

4. Add the remaining olive oil and heat for 1 minute. Add garlic and continue to cook.
5. When the onions are translucent, stir in the sausage pieces. Let cook for 1 minute to brown slightly.
6. Add in the salt and pepper, dry seasonings, bay leaves, thyme, carrots, celery, potatoes, split peas, and stock.
7. Bring to a boil, then simmer uncovered for 30 minutes.
8. Stir and skim off any foam.
9. Cook for another 30 minutes or until the peas are soft.
10. Stir frequently to keep the soup from sticking.
11. Remove from the heat and let cool. Discard the bay leaves and thyme sprigs.
12. When cool, add ½ of the batch of soup to a food processor or blender for 10 seconds.
13. Return the blended soup to the saucepot and combine with the unblended portion.
14. Bring to a boil.
15. Remove from the heat and let cool.
16. Ladle into bowls for serving.
17. Top the bowls with a dollop of coconut cream and the cooked bacon pieces.

Black Bean Soup

Since beans are naturally gluten free, free eaters can return to eating and actually being full after a hearty meal.

The secret to this recipe is cumin's earthy flavor, which unlocks the magic of this dish. Using freshly ground organic seeds and mixing them in with the chilis and spices make this dish a bold move for dinnertime.

Ingredients
1½ pounds dry black beans
1 bell pepper, diced
½ onion, diced
2 spicy chili peppers, seeded and diced (such as serrano)
10 to 12 cloves of garlic, minced
2 ribs of celery, minced
4 tablespoons cumin seeds, ground
4 tablespoons chili powder
2 tablespoons salt
1 tablespoon cayenne pepper, ground
1 tablespoon garlic powder
1 tablespoon onion powder
1 tablespoon black pepper, ground
1 whole tomato, diced
1 bay leaf
1 lime, juiced
Water (enough to cover the beans for soaking)
Stock (enough to cover the beans for cooking) plus 2 cups

Instructions

1. In a large pot, sort and wash the beans, and then drain. Remove any stones or debris.
2. Add the plain water, enough to cover 4 inches over the beans.
3. Cover the pot with a lid and soak the beans overnight. Drain to remove the soaking water.
4. Add all the chopped vegetables and dry spices to the pot.
5. When ready to cook, add stock or water to cover by 3 inches above beans.
6. Turn on to high heat and bring to a boil. Immediately reduce to low heat and simmer 2-3 hours.
7. Add the diced tomato and bay leaf.
8. Turn on to high heat and bring to a boil. Immediately reduce Low heat and simmer.
9. The beans should barely be bubbling and always cooking on a very slow boil.
10. Add 2 cups of stock. Continue to cook 4-6 hours until the beans are soft.
11. Discard bay leaf. Stir in lime juice.
12. To serve, ladle portions into bowls.

Lagniappe Variation
Garnish with shredded dairy-free cheese, tortilla strips, or avocado chunks.

BAKED EATS

Gluten-Free Bread Dough

Enjoy pizza, sweet buns, bagels, and all that again. Finally, gluten-free dough! Did I say, pizza crust? Um-hmm. Everybody's doing it; now top this!

Ingredients
1¼ cup dairy free or coconut milk (heated to 90°F)
½ cup coconut oil
1 large egg, at room temperature
¼ cup monk fruit sweetener granules
½ teaspoon salt
3½ cups gluten-free flour
2¼ teaspoon rapid yeast

Instructions
1. In a mixing bowl or stand mixer, add the dry mix ingredients. Set aside.
2. In another mixing bowl, add the dairy-free milk, oil, and egg. Whip to combine the liquid ingredients.
3. Slowly add a ¼ cup of flour at a time to liquid mix.
4. Mix until stiff yet slightly sticky. Slowly add more dairy-free milk if the dough is too crumbly.
5. Knead the dough on a gluten-free-flour dusted surface.
6. Put the dough back in the bowl.
7. Cover and let rise in a warm place for 1 hour. It may not double in size but will noticeably be a larger ball of dough.
8. Knead, cover and let rise again for 45 minutes before shaping, and use. Use the dough immediately.

Banana Oat Bread

Oats are known to be naturally gluten free. Take care, however, since oats are typically processed right alongside gluten-containing ingredients. Oats can be contaminated with gluten if good manufacturing practices are not used at the factory where they are processed.

I truly love to pack this hearty, sweet bread in the lunch box. I also take it on long road trips. You won't likely find a gluten-free alternative at a truck stop. Its dense goodness satisfies and keeps the hunger pangs at bay through every adventure.

Ingredients
1 cup packed brown monk fruit sweetener or brown monk fruit and allulose blend
½ cup vegetable oil
½ cup dairy-free milk, like coconut or cashew milk
2 large eggs
2 cups mashed ripe bananas (about 4 to 5 medium bananas)
2 cups gluten-free flour
½ cup raisins
1 cup old-fashioned oats
1 tablespoon baking powder
½ teaspoon baking soda
½ teaspoon cinnamon
Pinch of salt

Instructions

1. Preheat the oven to 350°F.
2. Grease a 9 × 5-inch loaf pan and dust with gluten-free flour or you can line the pan with parchment paper and then spray that with nonstick cooking spray instead.
3. In a large bowl, combine the brown monk fruit sweetener, vegetable oil, dairy-free milk of choice, and eggs. Mix until combined.
4. Stir in the bananas.
5. In a smaller bowl, combine the oats, flour, baking powder, baking soda, salt, and cinnamon.
6. Add the dry-ingredient blend to the wet ingredients all at once and stir until combined.
7. Pour the batter into the prepared loaf pan.
8. Transfer to the oven and bake until a toothpick inserted in the center comes out clean—about 50 to 60 minutes.
9. Let the loaf cool for 10 minutes before removing from the pan.
10. Let cool completely before cutting.

Cornbread

Cornbread is an absolute staple. My family enjoys it for breakfast when crumbled into vegan milk, as a grab-and-go snack, or as a quick and filling side dish at dinnertime. I welcome the fact that it is also a naturally fat-free grain.

Here is my best, sweet Cornbread recipe. This recipe will also be used as the starter batter for both my Spicy Hush Puppies and Apple Cornbread Stuffing.

Ingredients
1 cup corn meal
1 cup gluten-free flour
¼ cup monk fruit sweetener granules or monk fruit and allulose blend
1 tablespoon baking powder
½ teaspoon salt
1/3 cup dairy-free milk
1 large egg, slightly beaten
2 tablespoons zero-sugar honey alternative
Instructions
1. Preheat oven to 400°F. Grease an 8-inch square baking pan.
2. Mix all the dry ingredients in a bowl and set aside.
3. Combine all the liquid ingredients except 1 tablespoon of the zero-sugar honey alternative in a small bowl and stir to mix well.
4. Add the liquid ingredient mix to the dry ingredients and stir together until well blended.
5. Pour into the prepared baking pan. Drizzle the

remaining 1 tablespoon of zero-sugar honey
alternative on top of the mix before putting the pan
into the oven.

6. Bake for 20 to 25 minutes. To check if the cornbread
   is done, insert a wooden toothpick or knife into the
   center. If ready, it should come out clean.
7. Let cool or cut and serve warm.

Spicy Hush Puppies

Classic meals deserve to be paired with classic sides, like
Spicy Hush Puppies. Here's my gluten free version,
spiced up with fresh hot peppers. The key to fluffy and
light hush puppies is to let the batter rest for 15 minutes.

These are great to serve with fried dishes and Spicy
Sauce for dipping (see recipe).

Ingredients
1 batch of the prepared gluten-free Cornbread (see
recipe)
½ shredded onion
2 minced hot peppers (or substitute with ½ tablespoon
ground cayenne pepper)
½ cup dairy-free milk
Coconut oil, for frying

Instructions
1. Mix all the dry ingredients in a bowl and set aside.
2. Combine all the liquid ingredients except 1
    tablespoon of the zero-sugar honey alternative in a
    small bowl and stir to mix well.
3. Add the liquid ingredient mix to the dry ingredients
    and stir together until well blended.
4. Scoop by rounded tablespoons and fry the balls in a
    Dutch oven with hot coconut oil.
5. Fry until the hush puppies are ready when floating in
    the hot oil, then remove to let cool before serving.

Apple Cornbread Stuffing

Every day is a good day to celebrate yourself, family and friends. While some will come and go throughout life, homemade gluten- and dairy-free stuffing options are here to stay. You can simply make a baking pan batch of it or use as a stuffing for your dinner poultry. Either way, raise your hands and be counted, "More stuffing, please!"

Ingredients
1 gluten-free cornbread (see recipe)
½ cup oil, plus 4 tablespoons
1 large red apple, diced
2 ribs celery, diced
1 onion, minced
4 to 6 cloves of garlic, minced
1 cup stock
2 eggs
1 tablespoon sage
1 tablespoon thyme
½ tablespoon salt
4 tablespoons of zero-sugar honey substitute

Instructions
1. Prepare the gluten-free cornbread mix according to recipe instructions. Cook and let cool completely.
2. Crumble the cornbread into a large mixing bowl and set aside. Leave the oven on 350°F while preparing the rest of the recipe.
3. Melt 4 tablespoons of the oil in a pan over medium-low heat.

4. Add the apple, celery, onions and garlic to the pan.
5. Sauté for 5 minutes and remove from the heat.
6. Grease a 9 x 9 baking pan and set aside.
7. Add the sautéed vegetables to the crumbled cornbread in the mixing bowl.
8. Add the stock, egg, and dry ingredients. Fold the mixture gently.
9. Add the cornbread mixture to the greased baking pan. If you plan to use for stuffing, then gently fold to mix in a large bowl, then let rest for 5 minutes.
10. Melt the remaining ½ cup of oil. Do not boil.
11. Pour the melted oil over the ingredients in the baking pan or the large bowl for stuffing.
12. Drizzle the zero-sugar honey substitute over the top if you intend to bake it in a pan. If not, just drizzle over the ingredients in the bowl before you pack the stuffing loosely into the poultry and bake by following the meat cooking instructions.
13. Put the baking pan in the oven and let cook for 30 minutes.
14. Remove from the oven and let cool.

Peanut Butter Cookie Bars

Readers, who says free eaters can't have it all? You will find many popular dessert ingredients, like peanuts and some varieties of dark chocolate, are naturally gluten- and dairy-free. A quick warning, however: Momma's cookie bars are not safe when stored away.

Ingredients
1 large egg
½ cup monk fruit sweetener granules or monk fruit and allulose blend
¼ cup brown monk fruit sweetener (loosely packed)
¼ teaspoon vanilla extract
1 cup creamy peanut butter
Nonstick cooking spray

Instructions
1. Preheat the oven to 350°F.
2. In a mixing bowl, beat together the egg, sweeteners, and vanilla for about a minute.
3. Add the peanut butter. Beat until smooth.
4. Spray a baking pan with non-stick cooking spray.
5. Spread the mixture into the baking pan.
6. Bake for 15 to 20 minutes and insert a toothpick to determine if cooked. The cookie bar should be firm and slightly browned.
7. Transfer the pan of cookies to a baking rack and cool completely.
8. Cut into serving pieces.
9. Store in a sealed or lidded jar.

www.ingramcontent.com/pod-product-compliance
Lightning Source LLC
Chambersburg PA
CBHW061041050726
47592CB00004B/1538